Women Who Won't Be Silenced
The Stories of Strong Women

Ruth Bader Ginsburg

Lucent Press

Ellen Creager

Published in 2020 by
Lucent Press, an Imprint of Greenhaven Publishing, LLC
353 3rd Avenue
Suite 255
New York, NY 10010

Revised Edition

Developed and produced for Rosen by BlueApple*Works* Inc.

Managing Editor for BlueApple*Works*: Melissa McClellan
Designer: Tibor Choleva
Photo Research: Jane Reid
Editor: Marcia Abramson

Photo Credits: cover, p. 4, 49, 55 Steve Petteway, Collection of the Supreme Court of the United States/Public Domain; title page: Rob Crandall/Shutterstock.com; background Vladitto/Shutterstock; p. 7 Rob Crandall/Shutterstock.com; p. 8 David Shankbone/Creative Commons; p. 11 mark reinstein/ Alamy Stock Photo; p. 12 sach1tb/Creative Commons; p. 15 Olimpik/Shutterstock; p. 16 Nick Allen/Creative Commons; p. 17 Simmie Knox, under commission of the United States Supreme Court/Public Domain; p. 18 Beraldoleal/Creative Commons; p. 20 Lynn Gilbert/Creative Commons; p. 23 Kencf0618/Creative Commons; p. 24 Pete Souza/Obama Transition Team/Creative Commons; p. 26 Dmytro Zinkevych/Shutterstock; p. 27 David Dugan/Creative Commons p. 29 Rawpixel.com/Shutterstock; p. 30 Nancy Mao Smith/Shutterstock; p. 31 Chuck Kennedy (Executive Office of the President of the United States)/Public Domain; p. 32 Department of Defense. Department of the Navy. Naval Photographic Center/Public Domain; p. 34 US National Archives and Records Administration/Public Domain; p. 36–37 Rena Schild/Shutterstock; p. 38 Mgirardi/Creative Commons p. 39 Phil Roeder/Creative Commons p. 41, 43 Pete Souza/Executive Office of the President of the United States/Public Domain; p. 42 J. Louis Bryson/Shutterstock.com; p. 44 Pat Benic/Keystone Press; p. 45 Burlingham/Shutterstock; p. 47 Michael Brochstein/Keystone Press; p. 48 Executive Office of the President of the United States/Public Domain; p. 50 lev radin/Shutterstock.com; p. 51 jordanuhl7/Creative Commons p. 52 Ira Berger/Alamy Stock Photo; p. 56 Rob Crandall/Shutterstock.com

Cataloging-in-Publication-Data
Names: Creager, Ellen.
Title: Ruth Bader Ginsburg / Ellen Creager.
Description: New York : Lucent Press, 2019. | Series: Women who won't be silenced: the stories of strong women | Includes glossary and index.
Identifiers: ISBN 9781534566569 (pbk.) | ISBN 9781534566576 (library bound) | ISBN 9781534566583 (ebook)
Subjects: LCSH: Ginsburg, Ruth Bader--Juvenile literature. | United States. Supreme Court--Biography--Juvenile literature. | Judges--United States--Biography--Juvenile literature. | Women judges--United States--Biography--Juvenile literature.
Classification: LCC KF8745.G56 C743 2019 | DDC 347.73'2634 B--dc23

Manufactured in the United States of America

CPSIA Compliance Information: Batch #BW19KL: For Further Information contact: Greenhaven Publishing LLC, New York, New York at 1-844-317-7404.

CONTENTS

CHAPTER 1

WHO WAS RUTH BADER GINSBURG?

Ruth Bader Ginsburg was one of the most important figures in the history of the fight for women's rights in the United States. She became an associate justice of the U.S. Supreme Court in 1993. However, her life and legacy extended far beyond that role.

Dubbed “Notorious RBG” by her admirers, she has been the subject of not only books, but also T-shirts, tattoos, songs, an opera, and costumes for Halloween. In 2016, a new bug species was named after her. In 2018, filmmakers released two movies about her life—a documentary and a fictionalized account of her life and marriage.

However, the most important thing to know about Justice Ginsburg is that for six decades she worked to end sex discrimination. She knew the sting of discrimination firsthand. She was paid unequally to men. She had to juggle marriage, school, work, and motherhood. She was passed over and counted out. She just kept going, finding a way to succeed and create a fairer society.

She often was called “tiny” or “diminutive” because she was just 5 feet tall and 100 pounds. However, there was nothing small about her impact on the world. Ginsburg’s sharp brain, quiet calm, and great dignity buoyed her through a quarter of a century on the Supreme Court. She kept going through multiple bouts with cancer and through the death of her husband in 2010. She continued to work until her death in 2020, even working from her hospital bed at times.

When she died on September 18, 2020, the world lost a leading champion of equal rights. People flocked to the U.S. Supreme Court Building in Washington, D.C., to pay their respects to this icon of feminism. In addition, she became the first woman to lie in state in the U.S. Capitol, which is an honor reserved only for government officials who have left their mark as extraordinary citizens.

The legacy of "RBG" is one of strength, determination, and fierce feminism. She has inspired many people, especially women, to fight for what they believe in and to stand up for their rights and the rights of others.

"I DISSENT."

– Ruth Bader Ginsburg minority opinion on Bush v. Gore *case in 2000 that decided who would become president of the United States*

Young Ruth learned about the Jewish faith and studied the Hebrew language at East Midwood Jewish Center, a synagogue in Brooklyn. She was an honor student there, too!

CHAPTER 2

EARLY YEARS

She had a happy childhood, but it was not perfect. Joan Ruth Bader was born March 15, 1933. Her family was Jewish. Her mother, Celia, worked in a garment factory. Her father, Nathan, an immigrant from Russia, was a **furrier**. They lived in a modest apartment in Brooklyn, New York, in a neighborhood of Italian, Irish, and Jewish families.

When Ruth was a toddler, her older sister Marilyn, 6, died of meningitis. Ruth became an only child and the focus of her mother's attention. When she entered Brooklyn's Public School No. 238, teachers noticed right away that Ruth was very smart. She was an excellent student. At home, she read Nancy Drew detective books and liked poetry. With friends after school, she played jacks, rode bikes, and jumped rope. In the summers she went to Camp Che-Na-Wah in upstate New York.

In high school, she played the cello, was in booster club, and twirled the baton. Her best subjects at James Madison High School were English and history. Her worst were math and home economics. Her Jewish family was not very religious but celebrated traditions of Sabbath and the Jewish holidays.

Yet, outside events affected Ruth's happy childhood. When she was eight years old, the United States entered World War II against Germany and Japan, a scary event that affected everyone's life for the next four years. Then, when Ruth was 13, her mother fell ill. People in those days did not talk much about cancer, but Celia Bader had cervical cancer. She died in 1950, right before Ruth's high school graduation. Ruth missed her own graduation ceremony to help her father after the funeral.

> "THERE CAN BE A HAPPY WORLD AND THERE WILL BE ONCE AGAIN, WHEN MEN CREATE A STRONG BOND TOWARDS ONE ANOTHER, A BOND UNBREAKABLE BY A STUDIED PREJUDICE OR A PASSING CIRCUMSTANCE."
>
> *– Eighth grade essay by Ruth Bader Ginsburg, 1946, from the book* My Own Words

For some teens, a mother's death might derail their lives. For young Ruth, it did not. Instead, her mother's memory inspired her to succeed. In 1993, when she was introduced as the newest Supreme Court justice, she wore her mother's earrings. That day she thanked Celia Bader, recalling her as "the bravest and strongest person I have known, who was taken from me much too soon."

CHILDHOOD NICKNAME

Ruth Bader Ginsburg's childhood nickname was Kiki. Her actual given name was Joan Ruth Bader, but she was known as Ruth from a young age. When she grew up and married, she kept her original maiden name, Bader, and added her husband Martin's last name, Ginsburg. This confused many people in the 1960s and 1970s, even when she argued cases in front of the U.S. Supreme Court, where justices sometimes called her Mrs. Bader. Today, many people use hyphenated or multipart last names.

After she was sworn in, Justice Ginsburg gave thanks for the honor of serving on the court. She also thanked the female trailblazers who came before her in the American legal system.

Ruth chose to start her college studies at Cornell University in upstate New York, which had a place in women's history. In 1870, Cornell became one of the first U.S. colleges to admit women and allow them to attend classes with men.

CHAPTER 3

UNIVERSITY YEARS

Ruth knew that going to college had been her mother's dream for her, so in the fall of 1950 she entered Cornell University on an academic scholarship. There, she blossomed in her classes and social life.

At Cornell, she studied with two professors who taught her things that she would never forget. The Russian novelist Vladimir Nabokov taught her to write tightly and clearly, "to give people the picture in not too many words," she later told an interviewer.

The other professor, political scientist Robert Cushman, influenced her to declare government as her major and to think about going to law school. He inspired her to dream of improving society through the legal system.

"YOU FELT, WHETHER IT WAS TRUE OR NOT, THAT ALL EYES WERE ON YOU, THAT IF YOU GAVE THE WRONG ANSWER YOU WOULD FAIL NOT SIMPLY FOR YOURSELF BUT FOR ALL WOMEN."

– Ruth Bader Ginsburg on being only one of nine women in law school; interview in Columbia Journal of Gender and Law, *2013*

At the same time, she went on a date with fellow student Marty Ginsburg, 18. They became friends, then fell in love. They dreamed big – and his dreams included her career. They decided they should both go to law school. He started at Harvard Law School in 1953, and she was accepted for the following year.

However, life had other plans for the young couple. In 1954, Ruth graduated first in her class at Cornell. She and Marty got married. Then Marty was drafted by the U.S. Army and sent to Fort Sill, Oklahoma.

When Ruth looked for a job there, she took a government civil service exam and did well – until she mentioned she was pregnant. She was told she could be hired only for the lowest-level job as a claims adjuster. How would they get their dreams back on track? It would take hard work.

BACK AT HARVARD

In 1955, the Ginsburgs' daughter, Jane, was born. Still determined to go to law school together, the couple moved back north in 1956 to Cambridge, Massachusetts. It was rare for a woman to go to Harvard Law School in the 1950s. Ruth Bader Ginsburg's class had 500 men and only nine women!

THE STUDENT MOM

Ruth applied her determination and organizational skills to motherhood just as she did everything else. She later said that being the mother of baby Jane helped her succeed in law school. A nanny watched Jane during school days until Ruth came home about 4 o'clock and took over. "That was children's hour," Ruth said. "It was a total break in my day, and children's hour continued until Jane went to sleep. Then I was happy to go back to the books, so I felt each part of my life gave me respite from the other."

It's never easy to juggle babies and studies, but more moms do it today than in the 1950s. Just under half of colleges operate childcare centers to help out.

Harvard, the nation's oldest college, was male-dominated when RBG attended. In 2015, though, she was honored there for her transformative impact on society.

She did very well, but again, life did not go as planned. The young family faced a huge blow. In his final year of law school, Marty was diagnosed with testicular cancer, which at the time usually meant death. He got treatment, and Ruth arranged for their friends to take notes for him in his classes and even helped type his papers after her told her what to write. Amazingly, he got better and graduated on time.

Audiences sometimes asked Ginsburg why she always worked full-time, even when her children were little. She replied that due to her husband's cancer, she worried she might need to support her family alone and had to prepare.

GOOD AT MOST THINGS, BUT NOT ALL

Justice Ginsburg was a great jurist, but she was not good at everything. She loved opera, but she couldn't sing well. A teacher once told her she had the voice of a sparrow, and it wasn't a compliment. In addition, her husband Marty was the family cook after she botched many dinners. Her daughter Jane even once told an interviewer that her father did the cooking and her mother did the thinking. Young Ruth also reportedly failed her driver's test five times before passing. Luckily, as a Supreme Court justice, she got a car and driver.

This official portrait depicts Justice Ginsburg in 2000. It was painted by artist Simmie Knox.

COLUMBIA UNIVERSITY

Columbia University in New York City has played a big role in the lives of the Ginsburg family. It's one of the oldest universities in the United States – it was founded in 1754 as King's College under King George II of England. Its name was changed to Columbia after the American Revolution. Ruth Bader Ginsburg not only graduated first in her class at Columbia Law School, she taught there from 1972 to 1980. Martin Ginsburg also taught law at Columbia, from 1979 to 1980. And so does their daughter Jane! Ruth and Jane became the first mother and daughter to teach at the same U.S. law school.

In 1959, a healthy Marty got a job in New York, and Ruth did her final year of law school at Columbia University in Manhattan. She graduated first in her class. Then, she could not get a job. No one would hire a woman, even one as accomplished as she was.

Her professors asked Supreme Court Justice Felix Frankfurter to let Ginsburg **clerk** for him. He said he would not hire a woman. Neither would other judges or justices in the courts. One of the judges explained that he wanted to be able to swear when he felt like it, and a woman would be shocked by his bad language.

Finally, one of her professors told federal judge Edmund Palmieri that if he didn't take her on, he would never send him another graduate. Ginsburg then worked harder than any other clerk. Everyone saw what she could do. Suddenly, she got job offers.

But Ginsburg had other plans for herself.

"MY MOTHER WAS VERY STRONG ABOUT MY DOING WELL IN SCHOOL AND LIVING UP TO MY POTENTIAL. TWO THINGS WERE IMPORTANT TO HER AND SHE REPEATED THEM ENDLESSLY. ONE WAS TO 'BE A LADY,' AND THAT MEANT CONDUCT YOURSELF CIVILLY, DON'T LET EMOTIONS LIKE ANGER OR ENVY GET IN YOUR WAY. AND THE OTHER WAS TO BE INDEPENDENT, WHICH WAS AN UNUSUAL MESSAGE FOR MOTHERS OF THAT TIME TO BE GIVING THEIR DAUGHTERS."

– Ruth Bader Ginsburg, My Own Words

A 1977 photo by Lynn Gilbert captured Ginsburg in a reflective moment in her office during a time when she was both teaching law and fighting for **gender** equality.

CHAPTER 4

TEACHING AND ARGUING FOR GENDER EQUALITY

After a short stint in Sweden to study the legal system there, Ginsburg became a law professor at Rutgers University in New Jersey in 1963. While there, she became pregnant with her son James. This time, unlike in Oklahoma, she did not tell anyone she was pregnant until she had her teaching contract safely signed. She gave birth in early fall of 1965 and returned to work quickly.

At Rutgers, she began to focus on sex discrimination in the law. In 1970, she started a class called "Women and the Law." Such a class was a new idea. She found there were many laws that claimed to protect women but really discriminated against them. Some other laws were biased against men.

"SOMETIMES IT HELPS TO BE A LITTLE DEAF."

– Ruth Bader Ginsburg describing the best advice her mother-in-law gave her; used in many speeches and writings

One day, her husband showed her a small tax case that he thought might interest her. A single man, Charles Moritz of Denver, was not allowed to take a federal tax deduction for the money he spent to care for his elderly mother. Why? Only women and widowers could get the tax deduction. It was discrimination, plain and simple. With the help of the Ginsburgs, the courts threw out the rule.

"AS AN ADVOCATE IN GENDER DISCRIMINATION CASES IN THE SEVENTIES, I THOUGHT OF MYSELF AS AKIN TO A GRADE SCHOOL TEACHER. I WAS TALKING TO PEOPLE WHO REALLY DIDN'T UNDERSTAND ... THERE WAS DISCRIMINATION AGAINST WOMEN."

– Ruth Bader Ginsburg interview in Columbia Journal of Gender and Law, *2013*

In another case, *Reed v. Reed*, a disabled boy shot himself at his father's house. The mother, Sally Reed, applied to oversee her son's **estate**, but Idaho's law that "males are preferred" meant the boy's abusive father was named to handle his dead son's affairs. Ginsburg's 1970 brief to the Supreme Court helped get that law thrown out, too.

With these cases in the public eye, Ruth Bader Ginsburg's star began to rise. In 1972 she became the first **tenured** female professor at Columbia Law School in New York.

Sally Reed never became famous, but a historical marker in Boise, Idaho, honors her. Reed lived at the site of the marker for 64 years. The marker also honors the attorneys who fought on Reed's side for equality, including Ginsburg.

She also gained a position that would affect her life and those of women across America. She was co-founder and first director of the American Civil Liberties Union (ACLU) Women's Rights Project.

That group was looking for cases to bring to the U.S. Supreme Court that would challenge laws that treated men and women differently.

"DON'T TAKE NO FOR AN ANSWER, BUT ALSO DON'T REACT IN ANGER."

– Ruth Bader Ginsburg interview printed in Columbia Journal of Gender and Law, *2013*

5 THINGS THAT MIGHT SURPRISE YOU ABOUT RBG

1. She was left-handed.
2. In high school she twirled the baton.
3. She used to smoke.
4. On the Supreme Court she was best friends with conservative Justice Antonin Scalia, even though they disagreed on almost every case. He died in 2016.
5. She had a **stent** put in her heart in 2014. She also battled cancer multiple times before her death but worked with a personal trainer to stay as strong and healthy as possible.

FRONTIERO V. RICHARDSON

Today men and women receive equal benefits for their families when they serve in the U.S. military, thanks to *Frontiero v. Richardson.*

Brenda Feigen, who was co-director of the Women's Rights Project, recalled how brilliant Ginsburg was during the case. "There's no way to sound like I'm not in awe of her brain and ability to persuade people."

Feigen said Ginsburg didn't need to look at her notes about women's rights and history as she argued before the Supreme Court. "Not a single justice asked a question; I think they were mesmerized by her," Feigen said.

The Supreme Court building was finished in 1935. The statues represent Justice, left, a female, and Law, right, a male figure.

HER EARLY CASES

Today, some of Ginsburg's first cases seem so extreme that the average person would find them obviously wrong. But back in the 1970s, such discrimination was common.

In 1973, Ginsburg argued her first case before the Supreme Court, *Frontiero v. Richardson*. The Air Force refused to give a female lieutenant, Sharon Frontiero, the same housing allowance and health-care benefits for her husband that male service members got for their wives.

The Air Force reasoned that husbands should support wives, not vice versa. Ginsburg argued that such rules keep women in "a place inferior to that occupied by men in our society." She won the case.

Two other important cases she argued before the Supreme Court were:

- *Craig v. Boren* – a 1976 case challenging an Oklahoma law that let girls buy low-alcohol beer at 18 but boys not until 21. She won.
- *Duren v. Missouri* – a 1979 case challenging rules that kept most women off juries in some states. She won.

Ginsburg appeared six times in front of the U.S. Supreme Court and won five times. In total, she worked on 24 ACLU briefs for Supreme Court cases.

Her legal, step-by-step victories encouraged state legislators and Congress to treat women and men equally before the law and question any law that didn't.

"WOMEN WILL HAVE ACHIEVED TRUE EQUALITY WHEN MEN SHARE WITH THEM THE RESPONSIBILITY OF BRINGING UP THE NEXT GENERATION."

– Ruth Bader Ginsburg, in an interview with journalist Lynn Sherr

USING THE WORD "GENDER," NOT "SEX"

Most of Ruth Bader Ginsburg's legal briefs used the term "gender discrimination" instead of "sex discrimination." This was a decision, not an accident. Her secretary, who typed all the legal briefs, once pointed out that using the word "sex" over and over might distract male readers and listeners – that the word "sex" sounded too sexy. "Gender" was a less sensational word that still meant male and female.

Girls and women of all ages campaign for gender equality. Many have been inspired by Ginsburg.

WEINBERGER V. WIESENFELD

It was one of the most glaring gender discrimination cases that Ruth Bader Ginsburg argued before the U.S. Supreme Court.

Stephen Wiesenfeld's wife died in childbirth. He had to raise the baby on his own. When he applied for parental benefits from the Social Security Administration, they said only widows could collect, not widowers.

Her brief included the argument that even the baby was a victim of discrimination because the law "includes children with dead fathers but excludes children with dead mothers." In 1975, the Supreme Court struck down the law, ruling it was unconstitutional discrimination.

Why did Ginsburg take cases about men who faced discrimination? It helped judges and the public better understand similar bias against women.

RBG fought for gender equality throughout all of her long career.

The Women's Rights Project, of course, could not challenge all laws that were unfair. But they carefully chose cases that would steer the U.S. away from discrimination.

In 1974 Ginsburg and colleagues published a law school textbook, *Sex-Based Discrimination*. It was the first book of its type. She also helped fellow female employees at both Rutgers and Columbia file **class-action** lawsuits to gain equal pay and benefits. Even Ginsburg herself was paid less than some male professors.

Yet Ginsburg believed that you couldn't just change laws or rules or file suit. You had to change people's minds, too.

President Jimmy Carter wanted to make sure more women and minorities served as federal judges. He chose Ginsburg for the U.S. Court of Appeals.

CHAPTER 5

ON THE SUPREME COURT

In 1980, President Jimmy Carter appointed Ruth Bader Ginsburg to the U.S. Court of Appeals for the District of Columbia. There, she was a thoughtful federal judge who gained a reputation as a moderate.

Yet in the background, her husband and friends lobbied hard to get her name in the running for appointment to the U.S. Supreme Court, the highest court in the land. She had many powerful friends who wanted to see her succeed. Her intelligence made her one of the smartest judges in the nation. Her friends also believed her experience as a scholar and lawyer arguing discrimination cases before the court made her one of the most experienced candidates.

"JUDGES IN OUR SYSTEM ARE BOUND TO DECIDE CONCRETE CASES, NOT ABSTRACT ISSUES."

– Ruth Bader Ginsburg confirmation hearings statement in 1993, from the book My Own Words

For her swearing-in at the White House, Ginsburg used a Hebrew Bible held by her husband. Chief Justice William Rehnquist gave her the oath as President Bill Clinton watched.

That belief finally paid off. In 1993, President Bill Clinton nominated her to the U.S. Supreme Court. She prepared hard for confirmation hearings in the Senate, but the questions were friendly. The Senate easily approved her confirmation, 96-3. At age 60, she suddenly was the second woman on the U.S. Supreme Court.

She joined Justice Sandra Day O'Connor, who had been appointed in 1981 by President Ronald Reagan. Although O'Connor, from Arizona, came from a conservative Western background, and Ginsburg, from New York, came from a liberal Eastern background, the women became close colleagues. Two women on the court were better than one.

"WOMEN, I FULLY EXPECT, WILL – EVEN IN MY LIFETIME – COME TO SERVE THE CAUSE OF JUSTICE IN NUMBERS FULLY REFLECTIVE OF THEIR TALENT."

– Ruth Bader Ginsburg speech "The Supreme Court," April 2001

COURT DECISIONS

As the years went by, Ginsburg's biggest contributions to the Supreme Court were her keen questioning of attorneys and the writing of **majority and minority opinions**.

"PEOPLE ASK ME SOMETIMES... WHEN WILL THERE BE ENOUGH WOMEN ON THE COURT? AND MY ANSWER IS: WHEN THERE ARE NINE."

– Ruth Bader Ginsburg speech at Georgetown University, 2015

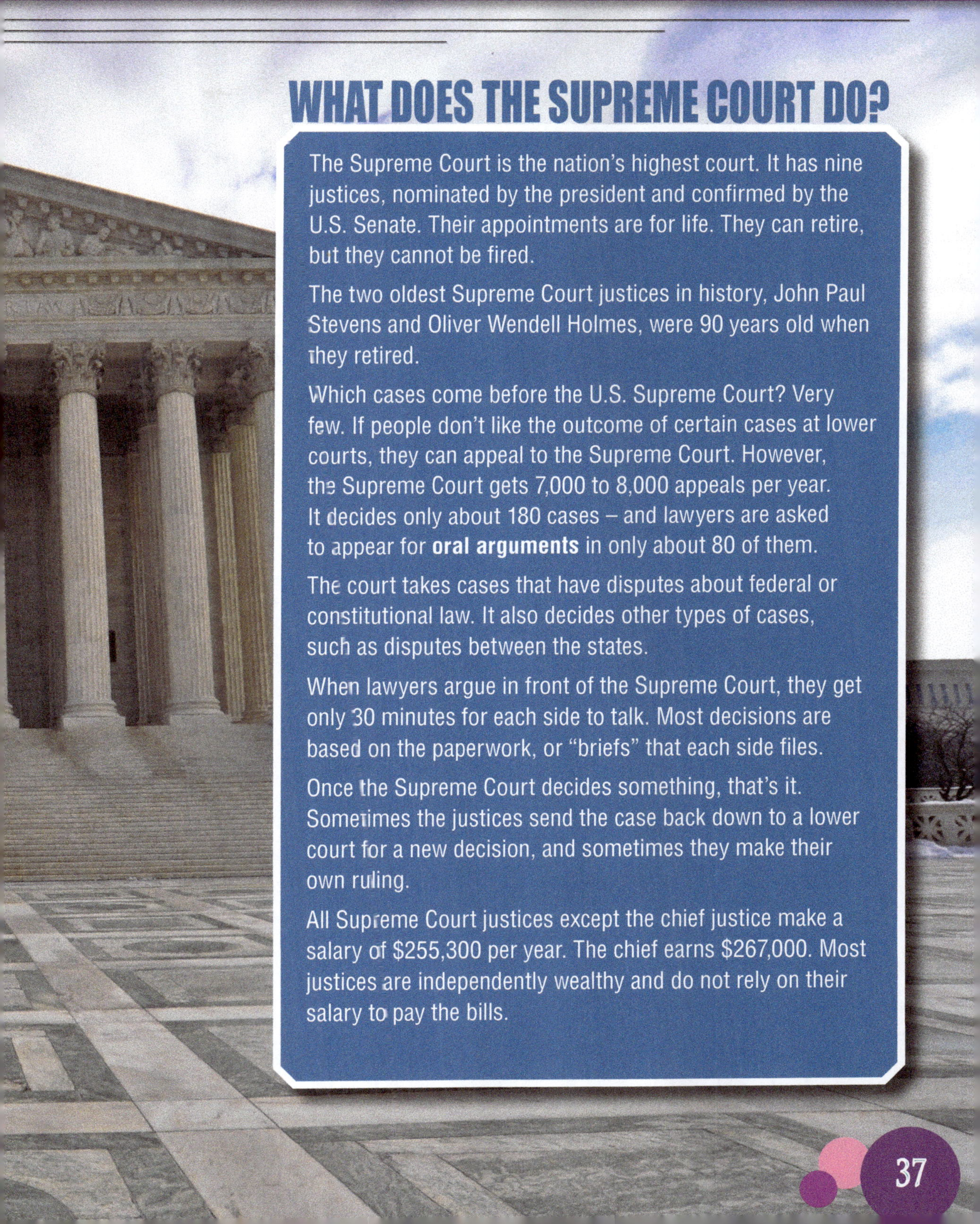

WHAT DOES THE SUPREME COURT DO?

The Supreme Court is the nation's highest court. It has nine justices, nominated by the president and confirmed by the U.S. Senate. Their appointments are for life. They can retire, but they cannot be fired.

The two oldest Supreme Court justices in history, John Paul Stevens and Oliver Wendell Holmes, were 90 years old when they retired.

Which cases come before the U.S. Supreme Court? Very few. If people don't like the outcome of certain cases at lower courts, they can appeal to the Supreme Court. However, the Supreme Court gets 7,000 to 8,000 appeals per year. It decides only about 180 cases – and lawyers are asked to appear for **oral arguments** in only about 80 of them.

The court takes cases that have disputes about federal or constitutional law. It also decides other types of cases, such as disputes between the states.

When lawyers argue in front of the Supreme Court, they get only 30 minutes for each side to talk. Most decisions are based on the paperwork, or "briefs" that each side files.

Once the Supreme Court decides something, that's it. Sometimes the justices send the case back down to a lower court for a new decision, and sometimes they make their own ruling.

All Supreme Court justices except the chief justice make a salary of $255,300 per year. The chief earns $267,000. Most justices are independently wealthy and do not rely on their salary to pay the bills.

Her most famous opinion for the court came in 1996. She was asked by the chief justice to write the majority opinion in a case called *United States v. Virginia*. It ruled that the Virginia Military Institute, long a male-only school, was required to admit women. Her words rang out: "We conclude that Virginia has shown no exceedingly persuasive justification for excluding all women from the citizen soldier training afforded by VMI." That ruling eventually changed how many colleges operated.

Women now can participate equally at Virginia Military Institute. More than 11 percent of the students are female.

HOT-BUTTON ISSUES BEFORE THE SUPREME COURT

Same-sex marriage: In 2015, Justice Ginsburg ruled with the majority in legalizing same-sex marriage in the United States. The case was called *Obergefell v. Hodges*.

Obamacare: In 2012, she ruled with the majority that the Affordable Care Act individual mandate to buy health insurance was constitutional but disagreed with another part of the ruling, saying some of the logic made "scant sense."

School searches: This 2009 case involved a middle school girl who was strip-searched for having ibuprofen. Ginsburg persuaded other justices to rule that school searches must take into consideration the age and sex of the student and the "nature of the infraction." She later told *USA Today* that her male colleagues did not quite understand the issue because they "have never been a thirteen-year-old girl."

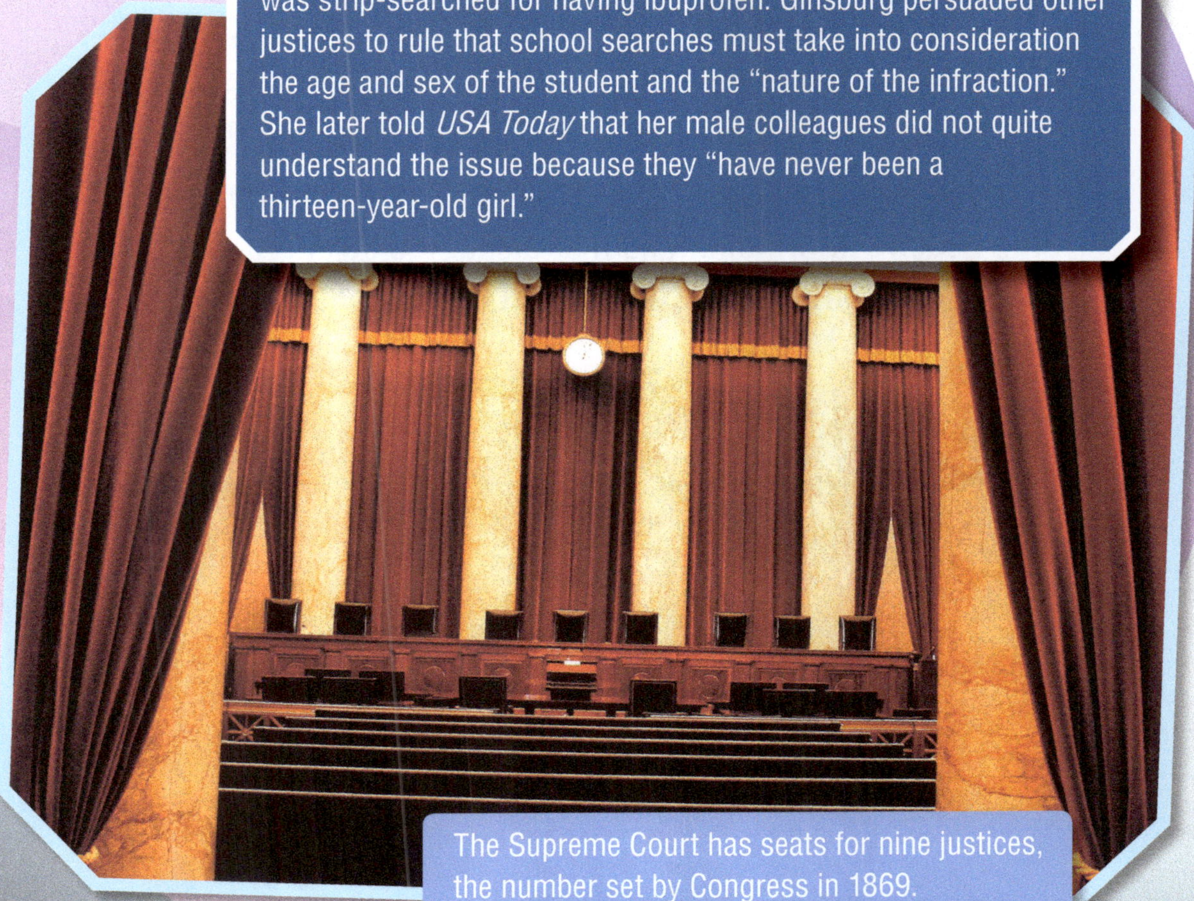

The Supreme Court has seats for nine justices, the number set by Congress in 1869.

Her work on the court was going well. Still, life had unexpected challenges.

In 1999, Ginsburg was diagnosed with colorectal cancer. She was treated with chemotherapy and radiation. She did not miss any work. Then in 2005, Justice O'Connor retired, leaving Ginsburg as the lone woman on the court. (She would have to wait until 2009 for another woman to be appointed – Sonia Sotomayor.)

In the meantime, President George W. Bush nominated two new conservative male justices. After that, Ginsburg found herself on the losing side of many important rulings.

In 2007, she started writing – and reading from the bench – more opinions that disagreed strongly with the majority opinions. These opinions are called **dissents**.

"DISSENTS SPEAK TO A FUTURE AGE. IT'S NOT SIMPLY TO SAY, 'MY COLLEAGUES ARE WRONG AND I WOULD DO IT THIS WAY.' BUT THE GREATEST DISSENTS DO BECOME COURT OPINIONS, AND GRADUALLY OVER TIME THEIR VIEWS BECOME THE DOMINANT VIEW."

– Ruth Bader Ginsburg, in an NPR interview, May 2, 2002

Sonia Sotomayor met with President Barack Obama, right, and Vice President Joe Biden in 2009 before her official nomination as the third woman on the Supreme Court. She and Ginsburg agreed on decisions about 90 percent of the time.

One of the biggest was in the 2007 Lilly Ledbetter case. It involved a woman who sued her employer after realizing she'd been discriminated against in pay for an entire decade. The Supreme Court ruled against her, saying she filed her case too late. Ginsburg read her dissent out loud, an unusual decision. Surely, she wrote, this is not what Congress intended. Congress must act so people could sue for long-term pay discrimination. Congress did act, in 2009, passing the Lilly Ledbetter Fair Pay Act.

Ginsburg would go on to dissent in other important cases on voting rights, abortion, and other issues.

LILLY LEDBETTER FAIR PAY ACT

Lilly Ledbetter was a supervisor for Goodyear Tire and Rubber in Gadsden, Alabama. After 19 years, she got an unsigned note telling her that she was making much less money than men with similar jobs. She sued the company for sex discrimination but lost in the Supreme Court because she did not file within 180 days of her first unfair paycheck – even hough she didn't know it was unfair for 19 years.

Justice Ginsburg urged Congress to prevent this from happening again. The Lilly Ledbetter Fair Pay Act was passed in 2009 as the first new law under new President Barack Obama. He was proud of the law, and so was Ginsburg, who kept a framed copy in her chambers. As for Ledbetter, she never got a settlement from Goodyear. But she said she was happy to make a difference for other women. Within a few years of the law's passage, hundreds had used it to achieve fair pay.

Although she had been ill, Justice Ginsburg attended the 2009 reception after Justice Sotomayor's swearing-in. She gave her a special gift: an elaborate white jabot.

SENIOR JUSTICE

In her 70s, she was urged by some advisers to retire so President Barack Obama could name a younger justice. She chose to stay on the court. However, she faced more personal hard times. In 2009, she had surgery to remove a small cancerous tumor in her **pancreas**. The surgery was a success. Two weeks later, she was back to work.

A year later, her husband, Marty, died, also of cancer. The next day, she was back **on the bench**.

In 2014, she had heart surgery. Again, her health problems did not stop her from returning to work quickly.

Justice Ginsburg got an escort to her seat at the 2017 inauguration of President Donald Trump.

Gradually, her more vocal dissents in court and her toughness in her personal life impressed admirers so much that her fame began to grow.

In 2013, after Ginsburg strongly dissented in an important case in which the Supreme Court weakened the Voting Rights Act, law student Shana Knizhnik started an admiring blog on the website Tumblr, called Notorious R.B.G. The name was a play on the name of a famous rapper, Notorious B.I.G. The quiet Supreme Court justice was about to turn into a media star.

THE VOTING RIGHTS ACT

The Voting Rights Act was passed in 1965 because some state and local officials were trying to keep minorities from voting long after the Civil War. Under the act, the federal government had to approve voting laws in areas with a history of discrimination. But by 2013, some states were saying the times had changed and the act was too strict. The Supreme Court agreed, by a 5-4 vote, that states no longer needed the advance federal approval.

Justice Ginsburg was one of the four who voted no. She wrote a famous dissent in which she said the ruling was like "throwing away your umbrella in a rainstorm because you are not getting wet." She cited numerous examples of voter discrimination in the twenty-first century. She warned that not only unfairness but chaos would result from the decision. And she was right. New laws were quickly passed that minority voters are challenging in the courts, and the issue of voting rights is far from settled.

Ginsburg first wore lacy gloves to protect her hands after chemotherapy. Then it became her style.

CHAPTER 6

OFF THE COURT

Justice Ginsburg had many interests besides the law. From an early age, she loved opera. She shared that love with her husband, Marty, and with fellow Supreme Court justice Antonin Scalia. She even appeared with Scalia on stage as non-singing opera extras. In 2015, a composer wrote a short, funny opera called *Scalia/Ginsburg* that contained this duet: "For our future is unclear, but one thing is constant – the Constitution we revere."

Ginsburg loved to travel, and she spoke at conferences around the world. She used to water-ski and play golf. She liked modern art. Justice Ginsburg was also known for her elegant fashion sense. She wore lacy collars with her judicial robes. When she was not working, she wore fashionable clothing, even gloves.

"IF I HAD ANY TALENT IN THE WORLD, ANY TALENT THAT GOD COULD GIVE ME, I WOULD BE A GREAT DIVA."

– Ruth Bader Ginsburg speech at Georgetown University, 2015

On and off the bench, Justice Ginsburg dressed up her outfits with many different styles of earrings and eyeglasses.

"She dresses with a dowager's elegance, often in exotic shifts acquired on her travels around the world," wrote court watcher Jeffrey Toobin in a profile of her for the *New Yorker* magazine in 2013.

Justice Ginsburg also might have been partly responsible for the renewed popularity of the scrunchie hair tie. It was last popular in the early 1990s, but the justice never stopped pulling her hair back in scrunchies.

Even in her 80s, she exercised regularly with a personal trainer. She could reportedly do 20 push-ups and get through a tough exercise routine.

JABOT COLLAR COLLECTION

When she first was appointed to the U.S. Supreme Court, Ruth Bader Ginsburg and fellow female Justice Sandra Day O'Connor adorned their plain black robes with white lacy collars, called jabots. Over time, the jabots got fancier.

Court watchers estimated that she had more than a dozen jabots. Some had glass beads, velvet, charms, or gold trim. Some were crocheted. Some had pearls and crystals. Women are not the only justices to adorn their robes. Former Supreme Court Chief Justice William Rehnquist had gold stripes on his robes.

#METOO MOVEMENT

When women around the world began speaking out in 2017 about sexual harassment at work, they gained power through their voices and actions.

Activist Tarana Burke (above) of New York has used the phrase "Me Too" since 2006 to encourage people to share their stories of sexual harassment. But it really caught on in 2017, when actress Alyssa Milano and others in Hollywood began speaking out and raising awareness.

Ruth Bader Ginsburg admired their courage. Asked about the #MeToo movement at a film festival in 2018, she said, "It's about time. For so long women were silent, thinking there was nothing you could do about it, but now the law is on the side of women, or men, who encounter harassment, and that's a good thing."

ABORTION RIGHTS MOVEMENT

In 1973, the Supreme Court made abortion legal in the United States in a case called *Roe v. Wade*. That case was decided 20 years before Justice Ginsburg joined the court. Still, she weighed in on the topic of abortion in her speeches and opinions.

One controversial speech she gave in 1993, the Madison Lecture, argued that *Roe v. Wade* had gone too far too soon, causing an angry national divide on the topic. Better if the law changed gradually, she reasoned, along with people's opinions.

However, as a Supreme Court justice, she was a strong defender of legal abortion. In 2016, the court struck down a Texas law that severely restricted abortion clinics. Her short but powerful opinion said that states that implement abortion restrictions that "do little or nothing for health, but rather strew impediments to abortion, cannot survive judicial scrutiny."

Fans can choose from more than a dozen styles of RBG coffee mugs, including this batch.

CHAPTER 7

RBG'S LEGACY

In her 80s, Ruth Bader Ginsburg found herself more famous than ever.

After Shana Knizhnik created the online blog about her in 2013, young people across the country became fans. Her fame then took on new forms:

- RBG coloring books, tattoos, and songs
- RBG costumes, popular for Halloween, including her big glasses, hair scrunchies, and gloves
- Two scientists in Cleveland named a new species of praying mantis bug after her, called "Ilomantis ginsburgae."
- The TV show *Saturday Night Live* has featured a comedian (Kate McKinnon) who plays the role of RBG.
- Her personal trainer wrote a book called *The RBG Workout* in 2017.

"I AM SOON TO BE 85, AND EVERYONE WANTS TO TAKE THEIR PICTURE WITH ME."

– Ruth Bader Ginsburg in a New York Times *interview, Feb. 8, 2018*

In addition to being a pop culture phenomenon, the justice continued to hear cases on the U.S. Supreme Court, writing opinions and asking sharp questions from the bench.

In February 2018 she told an audience at New York Law School that she still loved her work at the court and she wasn't going anywhere. She continued to serve on the Supreme Court for two more years, despite increasing numbers of health concerns. In 2018, she fell and broke multiple ribs. Following her fall, doctors discovered and treated cancer in her lungs. In 2019, she underwent treatment for pancreatic cancer once again. The disease ultimately led to her death on September 18, 2020.

"MY WRITING STYLE TENDS TO BE, SOME PEOPLE MIGHT THINK, MORE BLAND ... BUT I HOPE WHAT I WRITE HAS STAYING POWER."

– Ruth Bader Ginsburg interview printed in Columbia Journal of Gender and Law, *2013*

The death of Ruth Bader Ginsburg led to an outpouring of love from people around the world. Her legacy as an outspoken fighter for women's rights earned her many admirers, especially among young women. To them, "RBG" was a hero who helped change the world.

GREAT CHANGES

Women have made steady progress in the law since the 1950s, when Ruth Bader Ginsburg was one of nine women in a law school class of 500. Back then, only 3 percent of lawyers were women. By 2016, women made up more than 51 percent of law students. That's about the same as the percentage of women in the U.S. population.

As these students graduate, perhaps they will help raise the number of female judges, which is about 33 percent. That includes the Supreme Court, with three women out of nine at the time of Ginsburg's death.

When Elena Kagan, right, was sworn in to the Supreme Court in 2010, all the other women who ever served as justices attended. From left, they are Sandra Day O'Connor, Sonia Sotomayor, and RBG.

"I HAD THE GREAT GOOD FORTUNE TO MARRY A MAN WHO THOUGHT MY WORK WAS AS IMPORTANT AS HIS. THAT WAS RARE IN THE '50S."

– Ruth Bader Ginsburg interview printed in Columbia Journal of Gender and Law, *2013*

FAMILY LIFE

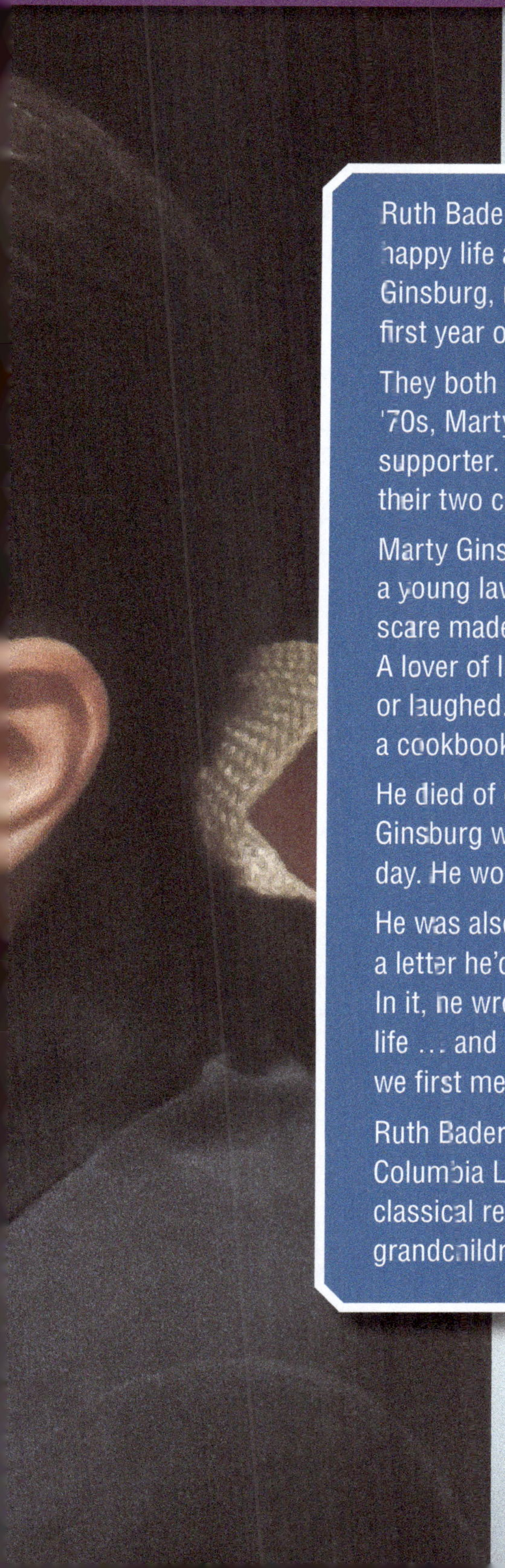

Ruth Bader Ginsburg's husband played a major role in her happy life and success in the law. Jolly and funny, Martin Ginsburg, nicknamed Marty, wooed her when they met in her first year of college at Cornell University. They married in 1954.

They both were lawyers. Unusual for couples in the 1960s and '70s, Marty Ginsburg promoted his wife's career as her biggest supporter. He also did the cooking at home and helped with their two children.

Marty Ginsburg got life-threatening cancer when he was a young law student. He was treated successfully, but that scare made the Ginsburgs treasure each other more than ever. A lover of life, he teased the quiet, serious judge until she smiled or laughed. They loved travel, opera, and he even wrote a cookbook.

He died of cancer on a summer Sunday in 2010. Justice Ginsburg was back on the bench at the Supreme Court the next day. He would have wanted it that way, their daughter said.

He was also a romantic. Just before his death, his wife found a letter he'd written to her in a drawer next to his hospital bed. In it, he wrote, "You are the only person I have loved in my life … and I have admired and loved you almost since the day we first met at Cornell some 56 years ago."

Ruth Bader Ginsburg had a daughter Jane, a professor at Columbia Law School, and a son James, president of a classical record label, Cedille, in Chicago. She also had four grandchildren. One of them, Clara, is a lawyer too.

RECOGNITION

Ruth Bader Ginsburg's achievements and honors include:

EDUCATION:

B.A. Cornell University, 1954

Attended Harvard Law School two years 1956-58

Law degree from Columbia Law School 1959

EMPLOYMENT:

Law clerk in the U.S. District Court for Southern District of New York 1959-61

Associate director of Columbia Law School Project on International Procedure 1961-63

Professor of Law, Rutgers University 1963-72

Professor of Law, Columbia University 1972-80

Judge, U.S. Court of Appeals for District of Columbia Circuit 1980-93

Associate Justice, U.S. Supreme Court 1993-2020

ACHIEVEMENTS:

Co-founder of *Women's Rights Law Reporter* journal, 1970

Co-founder and first director of Women's Rights Project, American Civil Liberties Union, ACLU general counsel, 1973-80

Argued six cases before the U.S. Supreme Court on gender equity, winning five, 1973-1979

More than 30 honorary degrees, multiple awards for her judicial work

Named one of *Time* magazine's "100 Most Influential People" in 2015

First woman to lie in state in the U.S. Capitol after her death in 2020

TIMELINE

1933
Born Joan Ruth Bader on March 15 in Brooklyn, N.Y. to mother Celia and father Nathan Bader

1950
Right before her high school graduation, her mother dies of cervical cancer

1954
Graduates from Cornell University. Marries Martin Ginsburg

1955
Daughter Jane born

1956-58
Attends Harvard Law School as one of only nine women. Husband gets cancer

1959
Transfers to Columbia Law School, graduates first in class

1959-61
Clerks for U.S. District Judge

1963-72
Becomes a professor at Rutgers Law School

1965
Son James born

1972-80
First female tenured professor at Columbia Law School; also first director of the ACLU Women's Rights Project

1973
Argues first case at U.S. Supreme Court, *Frontiero v. Richardson*, and wins

1980
Named federal appeals court judge for the District of Columbia

1993
Named by President Bill Clinton to the U.S. Supreme Court

1996
Writes majority opinion in *U.S. v. Virginia*

1999
Treated for colorectal cancer, returns to work

2009
Treated for pancreatic cancer, returns to work

2010
Husband Martin dies of cancer; she does not miss work

2013
Becomes a cultural icon when a law student starts an online blog, "Notorious R.B.G."

2014
Gets stent in heart, returns to work

2020
Dies on September 18 and lies in state in the U.S. Capitol

GLOSSARY

class-action: A type of lawsuit brought on behalf of a group of people who believe they have been harmed by the same person or organization.

clerk: To clerk for a judge is to work for them and assist with matters such as research, writing, and analysis.

dissent: To disagree. A minority opinion on the Supreme Court is sometimes called a dissent.

estate: The possessions someone leaves behind when they die.

furrier: A person who works with furs.

gender: Designation of male or female.

majority and minority opinion: Justices who are on the winning side of a case with the most votes write or sign the majority opinion. Those on the losing side may write or sign a minority opinion, or a dissent.

on the bench: A judge's seat on the court.

oral arguments: When a lawyer presents his or her case at court.

pancreas: Gland in abdomen that helps with digestion.

stent: A tube that is put in a blood vessel to keep it open, often in the heart.

tenured: When a professor is hired permanently and generally cannot be fired.

FOR MORE INFORMATION

BOOKS

Carmon, Irin and Shana Knizhnik. *Notorious RBG Young Readers' Edition: The Life and Times of Ruth Bader Ginsburg*. New York, NY: HarperCollins, 2017.

Ginsburg, Ruth Bader with Mary Hartnett and Wendy W. Williams. *My Own Words*. New York, NY: Simon & Schuster, 2016.

Kanefield, Teri. *Free to Be Ruth Bader Ginsburg: The Story of Women and Law.* San Francisco, CA: Armon Books, 2016.

WEBSITES

www.pbs.org/newshour/show/justice-ginsburg-enough-women-supreme-court

Watch Justice Ruth Bader Ginsburg speak at Georgetown University about what it's like to be one of only a handful of women to have ever served on the Supreme Court.

www.supremecourt.gov/about

Read about the Supreme Court of the United States.

INDEX